Selena Gómez

Actress and Singer / Actriz y cantante

Zella Williams

PowerKiDS press & Editorial Buenas Letras™
New York

Published in 2011 by The Rosen Publishing Group, Inc.
29 East 21st Street, New York, NY 10010

First Edition

Editor: Joanne Randolph
Book Design: Kate Laczynski
Photo Researcher: Jessica Gerweck
Spanish Translation: Eduardo Alamán

Photo Credits: Cover, pp. 1, 13 (top) Jason LaVeris/FilmMagic/Getty Images; pp. 4, 5 Theo Wargo/WireImage/Getty Images; pp. 6, 10 Jon Kopaloff/FilmMagic/Getty Images; p. 7 Michael Tran/FilmMagic/Getty Images; pp. 9, 20 Mathew Imaging/WireImage/Getty Images; p. 11 Mark Perlstein/Time & Life Pictures/Getty Images; pp. 12, 13 (bottom) Frederick M. Brown/Getty Images; p. 14 Todd Williamson/WireImage/Getty Images; p. 15 George Pimentel/WireImage/Getty Images; p. 16 Ray Tamarra/Getty Images; p. 17 Kevin Winter/Getty Images; p. 18 Mark Sullivan/WireImage/Getty Images; p. 19 Brian Ach/WireImage/Getty Images; p. 21 (top) Robert Benson/Getty Images; p. 21 (bottom) John Shearer/WireImage/Getty Images; p. 22 Jesse Grant/WireImage/Getty Images.

Library of Congress Cataloging-in-Publication Data

Williams, Zella.
Selena Gomez : actress and singer = actriz y cantante / Zella Williams. — 1st [bilingual] ed.
p. cm. — (Hispanic headliners = Hispanos en las noticias)
Includes webliography and index.
ISBN 978-1-4488-0715-4 (library binding)
1. Gomez, Selena, 1992—Juvenile literature. 2. Actors—United States–Biography—Juvenile literature. 3. Singers—United States—Biography—Juvenile literature. I. Title.
PN2287.G585W5518 2010
791.4302'8092—dc22
[B]

2010010383

Manufactured in the United States of America

CPSIA Compliance Information: Batch #WS10PK: For Further Information contact Rosen Publishing, New York, New York at 1-800-237-9932

CONTENTS

Meet Selena Gomez 4
Actress on the Rise 10
Singing, Charity, and More 16
Glossary 23
Index 24
Web Sites 24

CONTENIDO

Conoce a Selena Gómez 4
Actriz en ascenso 10
Cantar y compartir 16
Glosario 23
Índice 24
Páginas de Internet 24

Have you ever heard of Selena Gomez? If you have seen her work, then maybe you are a fan. She has played lots of parts on TV and in movies. She is best known for her work on *Wizards of Waverly Place*. She also sings in a band. She is just getting started, though. You may have heard some of her songs on the radio. If you have not heard of her yet, then you will!

Selena Gomez knew she wanted to become an actress at a young age.

Desde pequeña, Selena Gómez sabía que quería ser actriz.

Gomez is shown here with some of the other actors from *Wizards of Waverly Place*.

Aquí vemos a Gómez con algunos de los actores de *Wizards of Waverly Place*.

¿Conoces a Selena Gómez? Si conoces su trabajo quizás seas su admirador. Selena ha interpretado muchos **papeles** en el cine y la televisión. Selena es conocida por su trabajo en *Wizards of Waverly Place*. Pero también canta en una banda de música. Y esto es sólo el principio. Si no la has escuchado en la radio, seguro la escucharás muy pronto.

Selena Gomez was born on July 22, 1992, to Mandy Cornett and Ricardo Gomez. She was born in New York City. Soon her family moved to Grand Prairie, Texas, though. This is where Mandy Cornett's family lived. Mandy was only 16 when she had Selena. They did not have a lot of money during that time.

Selena's father, Ricardo Gomez, has family in Guadalajara, Jalisco, Mexico.

El papá de Selena, Ricardo Gómez, tiene familia en Guadalajara, Jalisco, México.

Mandy Cornett was also an actress. Now she helps her daughter in her acting career.

Mandy Cornett también fue actriz. Hoy ayuda a su hija en su carrera.

Selena Gómez es hija de Mandy Cornett y Ricardo Gómez. Selena nació el 22 de julio de 1992 en la ciudad de Nueva York. Cuando Selena era pequeña la familia se mudó a Grand Prairie, Texas, donde vivía la familia de su mamá. Mandy Cornett tuvo a Selena cuando tenía sólo 16 años. La familia no tenía mucho dinero en aquel tiempo.

Selena Gomez's parents **divorced** in 1997, when Selena was five. Her mother was an actress in the theater. Selena often went with her mother to **rehearsals**. It was during this time that Selena decided she would like to become an actress, too. Her wish came true sooner than she might have thought it would.

Gomez's mother married Brian Teefy, who became Gomez's stepfather, in 2006.

La mamá de Gómez se casó con Brian Teefy, que se convirtió en su padrastro, en 2006.

Los papás de Selena se **divorciaron** en 1997, cuando tenía cinco años. Su mamá era actriz de teatro. Con frecuencia, Selena iba con ella a sus **ensayos**. Fue durante estos días que Selena decidió que ella también quería ser actriz. Su deseo se hizo realidad antes de lo que ella esperaba.

When Selena turned seven, she got a **role** as Gianna on *Barney & Friends*. She appeared in this role many times. The shows did not air until she was in fifth grade, though. Over the next few years, she got more small parts. One of these parts was in *SpyKids 3-D: Game Over*, in 2003.

Once Selena got the part as Gianna, she started getting more parts.

Después de obtener el papel de Gianna, Selena comenzó a obtener más papeles.

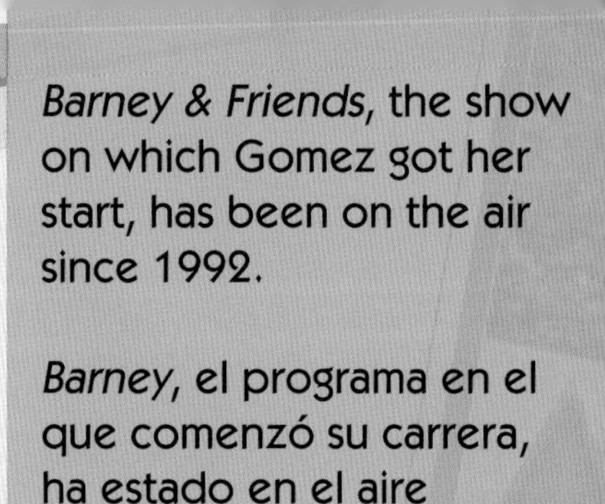

Barney & Friends, the show on which Gomez got her start, has been on the air since 1992.

Barney, el programa en el que comenzó su carrera, ha estado en el aire desde 1992.

A los siete años, Selena obtuvo el papel de Gianna en *Barney*. Selena apareció en este programa muchas veces. Estos programas no se transmitieron hasta que Selena estuvo en quinto grado. En los siguientes años, Selena obtuvo muchos otros papeles. Uno de estos fue en 2003, en *SpyKids 3-D: Game Over*.

In 2004, Selena Gomez started getting small parts on shows on the Disney Channel. She was in *The Suite Life of Zach & Cody* and *Hannah Montana*. Then, in 2007, Selena landed her own show. She took a part as Alex Russo on *Wizards of Waverly Place.* In this show, Alex and her brothers are learning to use their magical powers.

In 2009, *Wizards of Waverly Place* won an Emmy Award.

Wizards of Waverly Place ganó el premio Emmy en 2009.

Selena comenzó a obtener pequeñas partes en el canal de Disney en 2004. Selena estuvo en *The Suite Life of Zach & Cody* y en *Hannah Montana*. En 2007, Selena consiguió su propio programa, en el papel de Alex Russo en *Wizards of Waverly Place.* En este programa, Alex y sus hermanos tienen poderes mágicos.

One of Gomez's costars on *Wizards of Waverly Place* is Jake T. Austin, shown with her here.

Aquí vemos a Gómez con su compañero Jake T. Austin de *Wizards of Waverly Place.*

The actors on *Wizards of Waverly Place* are giving a talk about their show here.

Aquí los actores de *Wizards of Waverly Place* hablan acerca de su programa.

In 2008, Selena Gomez took a part in *Another Cinderella Story*. She also had movie roles in *Princess Protection Program* and *Wizards of Waverly Place: The Movie*. In 2009, she got a part in *Ramona and Beezus*, based on a book by Beverly Cleary. She has done some voice acting for movies, too, including *Horton Hears a Who!*

Gomez and her friend Taylor Swift during a showing of *Another Cinderella Story*.

Gómez y su amiga Taylor Swift durante una presentación de *Another Cinderella Story*.

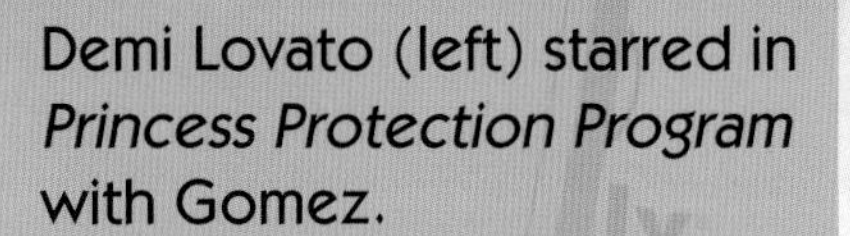

Demi Lovato (left) starred in *Princess Protection Program* with Gomez.

Demi Lovato (izquierda) actuó con Gómez en *Princess Protection Program.*

En 2008, Selena actuó en *Another Cinderella Story*. Además tuvo papeles en *Princess Protection Program* y la película de *Wizards of Waverly Place.* En 2009, obtuvo un papel en *Ramona and Beezus*, que se basó en un libro de Beverly Cleary. ¡Además, Selena ha prestado su voz para el cine, como en la película *Horton Hears a Who!*

Selena Gomez does more than act. She also sings and dances. In 2008, she started a band called Selena Gomez & the Scene. The band's first album came out in September 2009. It is called *Kiss & Tell*. It sold 66,000 copies in the first week! Gomez has also recorded songs for some movie sound tracks. Some of these were for movies she had a part in but some were not.

Gomez sang a song from her first album on a TV talk show called *Good Morning America*.

Gómez canta una canción de su primer álbum en el programa de televisión *Good Morning America*.

Here Selena Gomez & the Scene play in Las Vegas on New Year's Eve 2009.

Aquí, Selena Gómez & the Scene tocan en Las Vegas durante el Año Nuevo 2009.

Selena Gómez no sólo actúa. Selena también canta y baila. En 2008, comenzó una banda llamada Selena Gómez & the Scene. Su primer disco salió en septiembre de 2009. Se llama *Kiss & Tell*. En la primera semana vendió 66,000 copias. Además, Gómez ha grabado canciones para algunas películas. Selena ha actuado en algunas de estas películas.

Selena Gomez also does a lot of **charity** work. She helped in the UR Votes Count **campaign** in 2008. This campaign tried to get young people to learn more about presidential candidates. It also encouraged them to vote. She was named one of UNICEF's goodwill **ambassadors** in 2009.

A young girl gave Gomez this card at a UR Votes Count event.

Una chica le dió a Gómez esta tarjeta en un evento de UR Votes Count.

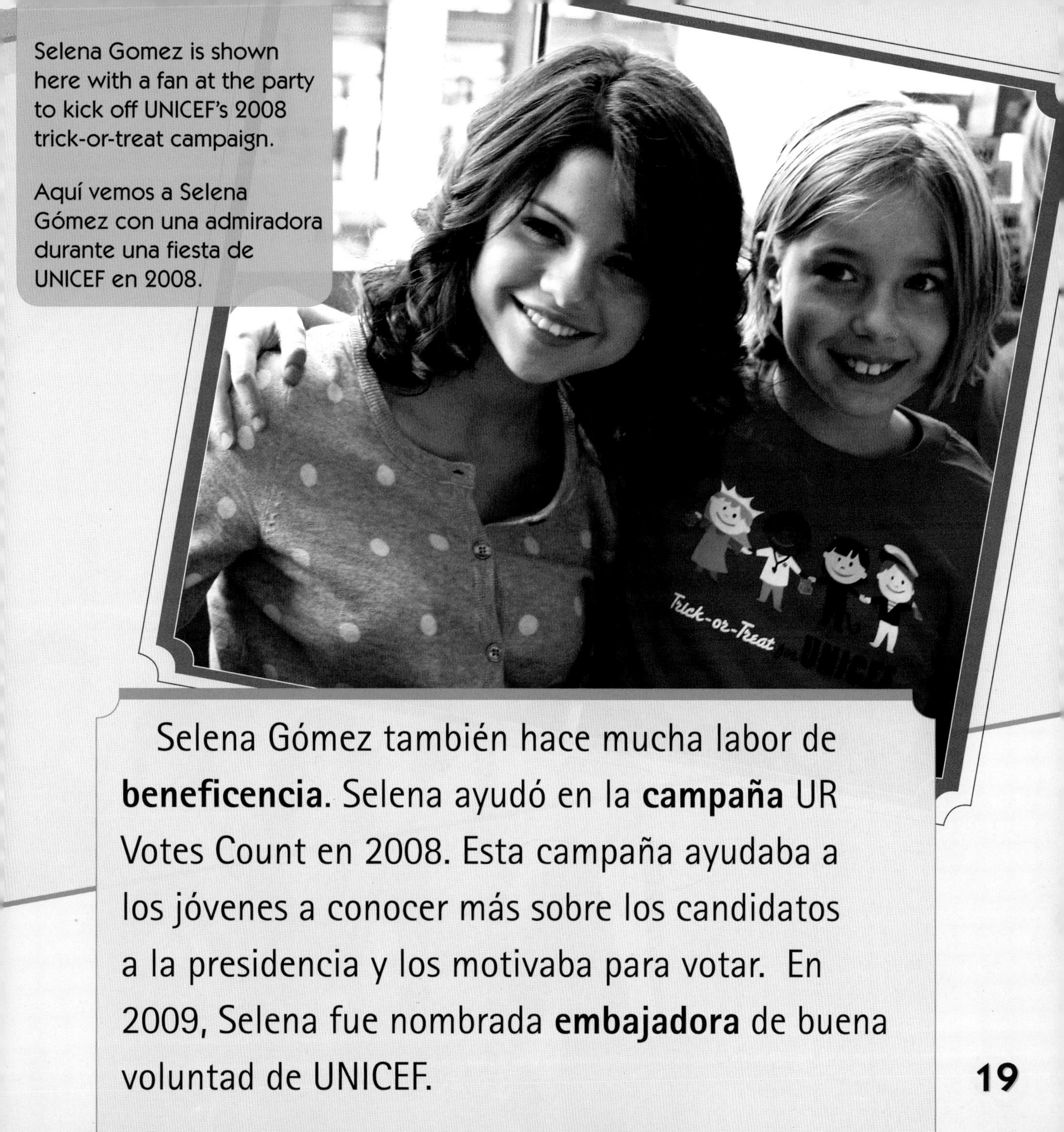

Selena Gomez is shown here with a fan at the party to kick off UNICEF's 2008 trick-or-treat campaign.

Aquí vemos a Selena Gómez con una admiradora durante una fiesta de UNICEF en 2008.

Selena Gómez también hace mucha labor de **beneficencia**. Selena ayudó en la **campaña** UR Votes Count en 2008. Esta campaña ayudaba a los jóvenes a conocer más sobre los candidatos a la presidencia y los motivaba para votar. En 2009, Selena fue nombrada **embajadora** de buena voluntad de UNICEF.

Selena Gomez has been **nominated** for and won many awards for her work. She won a Kid's Choice Award in 2009 for *Wizards of Waverly Place*. She won some Teen Choice Awards that year, too. She has also been nominated for Alma and Imagen awards for her work as a Latina artist.

Here the actors from *Wizards of Waverly Place* show off their Emmy Awards.

Aquí vemos a los actores de *Wizards of Waverly Place* mostrando sus premios Emmy.

Selena Gómez ha ganado muchos premios. Selena ganó el Kid's Choice Award en 2009 por *Wizards of Waverly Place*. Ese año también ganó algunos Teen Choice Awards. Además ha sido **nominada** para los premios Alma e Imagen por su trabajo como artista latina.

Selena Gomez is shown here thanking people for her 2009 Alma Award.

Selena Gómez agradece por su premio Alma en 2009.

Here Gomez receives her 2009 Teen Choice Award.

Aquí Gómez recibe su Teen Choice Award en 2009.

We are sure to see a lot more from Selena Gomez. She already has her own production company, called July Moon Productions. She also has a clothing line, called Dream Out Loud by Selena Gomez. What else will she do? The sky is the limit for this young actress and singer!

Seguramente veremos mucho más de Selena Gómez. Selena ya tiene su propia casa productora, llamada July Moon Productions. También tiene una marca de ropa llamada Dream Out Loud por Selena Gómez. ¿Qué más podría hacer Selena? ¡Para esta joven estrella el cielo es el límite!

GLOSSARY

ambassadors (am-BA-suh-durz) People who are voices for countries or groups and who visit other countries or groups to share a message.

campaign (kam-PAYN) A plan to get a certain result, such as to win an election.

charity (CHER-uh-tee) A generous act.

divorced (dih-VORST) Ended a marriage.

nominated (NO-muh-nayt-ed) Picked to do a certain job.

rehearsals (rih-HER-sulz) Practices for something, such as a play.

role (ROHL) A part played by a person or thing.

GLOSARIO

beneficencia Un acto de generosidad.

campaña (la) Un plan para obtener un resultado.

divorcio (el) Terminar un matrimonio.

embajadora (la) Una persona que representa a un grupo o país para visitar otros países para transmitir un mensaje.

ensayos (los) Practicar para algo, como una obra de teatro.

nominada Ser elegida para una posición u honor.

papel (el) La parte representada por una persona.

INDEX

A
award(s), 20

B
band, 4, 16

C
Cornett, Mandy (mother), 6, 8

F
family, 6
fan, 4

G
Gomez, Ricardo (father), 6

M
movies, 4, 14, 16

P
part(s), 4, 10, 12, 14, 16

R
role(s), 10, 14

T
theater, 8

W
Wizards of Waverly Place, 4, 12, 20

ÍNDICE

A
admirador, 5

B
banda, 5, 17

C
Cornett, Mandy (madre), 7, 9

F
familia, 7

G
Gómez, Ricardo (padre), 7

P
papel(es), 5, 11, 13, 15
parte(s), 13
película(s), 15, 17
premio(s), 21

T
teatro, 9

W
Wizards of Waverly Place, 5, 13, 21

WEB SITES / PÁGINAS DE INTERNET

Due to the changing nature of Internet links, PowerKids Press and Editorial Buenas Letras have developed an online list of Web sites related to the subject of this book. This site is updated regularly. Please use this link to access the list:
www.powerkidslinks.com/hh/gomez/